THE
POLKA-DOTTED
POSTMAN

AND OTHER STORIES

A Celebration of
Unusual Minds

THE POLKA-DOTTED POSTMAN

AND OTHER STORIES

BOB BIDERMAN

illustrations by CAT WEBB

BLACK
APOLLO
PRESS

First published in Great Britain by
Black Apollo Press,
Germinal Productions, Ltd , 2012

ISBN: 9781906448080

A CIP catalogue record of this book is available at the
British Library.

For information regarding our other titles, please go to
our website:
www.blackapollo.com

Contents

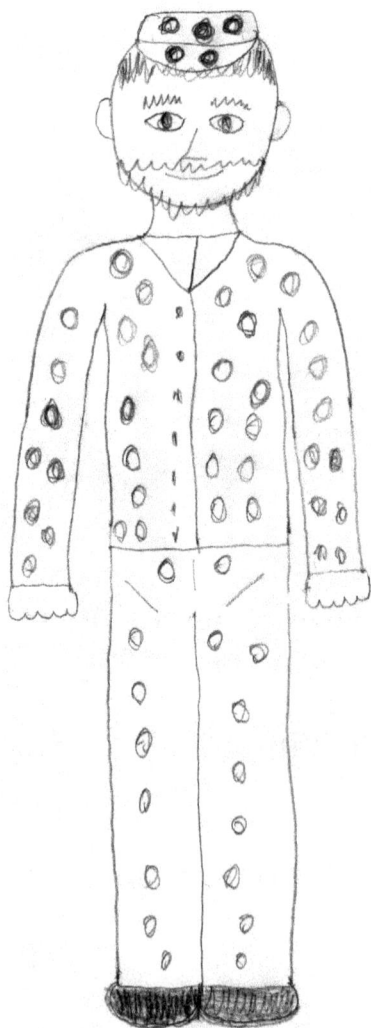

The Polka-Dotted Postman

He always wore polka dots – a polka dot shirt, polka dot trousers, polka dot tie and polka dot socks. Except for that he dressed in standard postal uniform. I'm not sure how he got away with it – even though the polka dots were stick-ons that he probably fixed to his clothes after he left the sorting office. And he may well have de-polka-dotted himself after his deliveries were done before coming back to clock off at the end of his day.

I once asked him why he went to all that trouble for over fifteen years. He said I was the first one to ever question him about it. I have my doubts. It's hard to believe that nobody else had ever asked him why he did such a ridiculous thing. But who knows? Maybe the other people on his route were just happy to receive their mail and as long as he was regular as clockwork – which he was – they were willing to accept some harmless nonsense like wearing inappropriate dots on his clothing. Perhaps they were too embarrassed to ask - though, more likely, they probably felt that if he were rubbed the wrong way maybe some important piece of mail they were expecting would somehow go missing.

Besides, as I said, he was a pretty good postman – steady and reliable. He'd go out of his way to re-deliver a package if no one was home the first time and – as I found out later - he'd even dig into his own pocket if there was postage due and he knew the person the letter or package was meant for was going through some difficulties. (Mailmen do get to know quite a bit about the lives and loves of the people on their route which, of course, is understandable considering how many of us actually write an extensive and sometimes very personal PS on the back of the envelope prior to posting because we'd forgotten to write something we deemed very important and the letter was already sealed.)

I once saw him really upset, though. A dog had snatched one of his polka dots right off him and had scampered away. When I had come along, the dog was across the street, clutching the polka dot in its teeth and staring at the postman as if daring him to retrieve it.

'It was my favourite,' the postman told me. He looked forlorn, as if he had indeed lost something very dear to him.

'Aren't you going to try to get it back?' I asked.

'Actually, I'm afraid of dogs,' he admitted.

'But that one's wagging its tail,' I said.

'I know that dog,' he said, looking at the mutt suspiciously. 'We don't get along much any more...'

The mutt (and mutt it was - a mixture of at least twenty breeds I imagine) had cocked its head to one side in a playful manner. Its stub of a tail was wagging furiously and its pointy ears were stiff and erect as if anticipating something quite pleasurable.

'It wants to play,' I said. 'It probably thinks your polka dot is a deflated ball. Dogs can't see dimensionally, you know.'

'They can't?' he said, transferring his gaze from the dog to me, but this time instead of an exclamation

11

point, his eyes contained a question mark writ bold.

Actually, I had no idea whether a dog can see dimensionally or not. Maybe they do, maybe they don't. Maybe they skip the third and go on to the fourth. What I had said just slipped out of my mouth. I guess I was trying to mediate between the world of dogs and polka dotted postmen. But it's not an easy thing reconciling a recalcitrant woofer and a po-faced clown.

I did try to get the errant polka-dot back for him. I crossed the road, attempting to stare the little mongrel down. It let me get about two strides from its prize – its deflated, two-dimensional ball – before it took off, scampering into the distant unknown.

That was the last I saw of them - both the dog and the polka-dotted postman. Three days later, after not receiving my mail, I rang the post office to see what was up.

'Maybe no one's written you,' said the supervisor after I had been passed around from hither to yon through the maze of electronic beeps and whistles that make up the modern communications system, guaranteeing nobody speaks to anyone who knows anything beyond a simple list of frequently asked questions that you probably could find on your computer anyway. Besides, how could anyone answer a question sensibly when everything has to be categorised in boxes numbered one, two, three or four, the button for which you have to press at the sound of the tone? And what number do you press to find out about your polka-dotted postman?

'None of my neighbours received their mail either,' I replied.

'The mail's slow this time of year,' the supervisor said.

'What time of year isn't it slow?' I asked.

I could hear him sigh on the other end the line. It seemed to me like the air seeping out of a deflating polka-dot. 'I'll look into it and get back to you,' he said.

Amazingly, I did hear from the postal supervisor a few days later. It was after a week of not receiving any mail.

'I'm sorry to tell you this,' he said, 'but your postman is dead.'

'What?' I replied unbelievingly. 'Are you sure you're talking about my postman? I saw him just a few days ago and he seemed perfectly fit.'

Of course, I didn't mention the circumstances in which I saw him last. I didn't think the supervisor needed to know about my postman's strange obsession – even if he were dead. Especially if he were dead, in fact, as you never know how things like this affect insurance policies, pension rights and so on.

'Are you absolutely certain you're speaking about my postman?' I asked again.

He had me confirm my name and address and then said, 'Yes, Mr. Barboosh has been the postman on that route for fifteen years. It seems he died unexpectedly...'

'When is death ever expected?' I asked.

'There are occasions,' he replied. 'An elderly man with a bad heart condition and advanced diabetes, for example.'

'I wouldn't have thought my postman had a heart condition considering his gruelling routine,' I replied. "I've never done anything like that myself, but I'm sure his work wasn't easy. And I don't remember him ever taking a holiday unless he took it the same time I took mine.'

'His record does appear to have been exemplary,' the supervisor confirmed. 'There wasn't any indication of ill health – it seems he hadn't even taken any sick days....'

'Thinking about it, I did have an uncle who popped off one day without rhyme or reason,' I said, recalling that death could indeed be quite an arbitrary reaper.

'There you have it,' said the supervisor. 'You just don't know about these things, do you?'

'No,' I agreed. 'You never know. And if you did, you probably wouldn't want to.'

'Want to what?' he asked.

'To know when someone is going to be dead before it happens.'

There was a brief silence on the other end of the line. Then he said, 'I suppose you're right. Knowledge like that would present all sort of problems.'

We went on like this for several minutes. In a strange way, we sort of connected. I'm not a great one for telephone relationships but I guess both of us found a bit of solace through the disconnected voices of strangers communicating simple philosophies of life that maybe take the edge off the grim realities of non-existence.

In the end we decided to continue our conversation at a neighbourhood watering hole after work. Curiously, I recognised him right away. And he said, later, he had recognised me. Strange how those things happen, isn't it? How can you match a face to a voice? I think it was his eyes. They were a mixture of dire boredom from being a bureaucrat far too long and another layer, just beyond, that spoke of kings and cabbages.

We became something like, but not quite, friends that evening – though chummy enough to meet up several times afterwards. It was at the third meeting, I think, that he told me. 'You know,' he said, 'there was something strange about Mr. Barbo-osh – your postman…'

'Yes,' I replied. 'He was slightly odd, wasn't he?'

'You knew?' he said, looking at me amazed.

I was struck by his amazement. 'All you had to do was look at him,' said I.

The supervisor took a drink of his warmish beer. 'You must have a keen eye for character,' he said.

'How so?'

'For being able to see beyond the man…'

'Perhaps we're speaking of differ-ent things,' I admitted. 'You aren't referring to his polka-dots?'

'Polka-dots? I know nothing of

polka-dots.' He took another drink of beer and then he said, 'Actually I do.'

'Do what?

'Know something about polka-dots. I'm a crossword aficionado, you see. I spent weeks suffering over a clue that read – "zits on your bottom".'

'Polka-dots?'

He nodded. 'Sometimes you get odd clues like that and it drives you bonkers. Are you a crossword man?' he asked, looking at me hopefully.

I shook my head.

He gazed down at his suds. 'Mr Barboosh was a complicated post-man...'

'Yes he was,' I agreed.

"He died at home, you know. Alone...'

'How sad.'

'Very sad indeed.'

'How did they find him?' I asked.

'A neighbour noticed he hadn't come down to smell the petunias in his garden. He had a very strict routine, she said. You could tell the time by his movements.'

'Which made him a good post-man,' I said.

'Yes,' the supervisor agreed, 'except for one thing...' His voice trailed off as if he had entered a different flow in the tidal stream of memory and imagination.

'Except for one thing?' I prompted him.

The supervisor looked at me with tired eyes, splotched with narrow lines of red that gave the impression of marble balls under such pressure they had started to show signs of hairline fracturing. 'He did something no postman should ever do – something unforgivable,' he said.

I tried to think what could possibly be so dire that the supervisor would consider it "unforgivable".

'He was opening the mail,' the supervisor said, answering my unspoken question.

'Opening the mail?' I repeated, scarcely believing I heard correctly. 'How can you be certain?'

'It was all in the police report. All very neat and tidy. He was found slumped in his chair. On the table before him were stacks of letters which had been steamed open and were waiting to be resealed.'

'He was searching for money?'

'There's no evidence of that,' the supervisor said. 'No one has report-ed missing cheques or funds that have been stolen.'

'Perhaps he hadn't found anything worth stealing. It's not a wealthy neighbourhood,' I said.

'What's strange is one of the letters that had been opened did contain some cash. But it had been neatly folded back inside the envelope.'

'How very curious,' I said.

'Stranger still,' said the supervisor, 'there's some evidence he had actually put his own cash into letters that contained none before.'

'You don't say!'

'He even seemed to have been forging the mail...'

'How so?'

'One of the letters he'd been adjusting when he was found was a rather brutish goodbye to a woman from an ex-boyfriend. Our friend seemed to have added a little addendum that moderated the brusqueness – something like "you deserved better and one day your prince will come", something like that. And then he stuck in a little cash with a note which read, "a little token to say how sorry I am for treating you unkindly..."'

'That doesn't sound so bad,' I said.

'Maybe not but it's a crime to open letters. Postmen can't play God.'

'No,' I said. 'I suppose not.'

Some days later I was speaking with one of the elderly women who lives on the ground floor of my building and I asked her about the polka-dotted postman.

'He was a very good postman,' she said.

'Yes, he was,' I agreed.

'He always brought the mail on time,' she said. 'Nowadays we're lucky if we get our mail at all.'

'Did you know him – I mean, did you ever speak with him?' I asked.

'Just to say "hello", she said. 'He was a very friendly postman but he kept to himself, didn't he?'

I rang the supervisor again that evening. 'Did he have any family?' I asked.

'None that we know of.'

'What happened to the body?'

'It was taken to the morgue, I guess.'

'Was there a funeral?'

'The post office doesn't do funerals,' he said.

That night I had a dream. I dreamt that there had been a funeral parade for our postman. The road was lined in polka dots. The hearse that carried his body was covered in polka dots. And everyone in the neighbourhood who had come to pay their respects was dressed in polka-dots.

Many months later I managed to track down where the postman had been buried. As it turned out, he did have a sister somewhere who had seen to the arrangements.

The grave of Mr. Herman Barbo-osh was stuck away in the corner of a ramshackle cemetery covered in weeds and vines. When I found it I cut away the bracken and then took from my pocket some plastic polka-dots which I glued to the marble slab that marked his final resting spot.

The Salesman

The old wooden door had been recently painted. Green. Olive green. Olive, though, might have been a bad comparison. Olives, to him, were deliciously transcendent. The food of the gods. The colour of the door was stomach-churningly putrid. Or so he thought as he brought his knuckles close enough to knock, close enough to feel the radiant chill of the wood tingle through his skin even though his fist was still several millimetres from actually touching it. He hesitated, turning his head in the direction of a nearby sound. The sound was that of a cat, scurrying from beneath a bush – it was too dark to specify the genus of either the feline or the plant – which made him feel nervous. His stomach tightened. The cat, he thought, was black - though he couldn't be certain because the evening light was dim and colours were starting to fade. He had a problem with colours anyway. Blues and greens in particular. Sometimes. The door was definitely green. Putrid green. Putrid greens he saw. He not only saw, he felt them in the pit of his stomach. Colours often had a visceral affect on him. He knew what he saw and he knew what he felt, it's just that he sometimes confused them. Or other people did. He couldn't be certain.

Why was he wrong and they right? Just because people said he was mistaken didn't mean he actually was. It was all a question of percentages – as were most things in life. A percentage of people saw blue as green and green as blue. Not many but some. But who's to say they were wrong? Why was he wrong just because he was in the minority? On the other hand, anyone would have had trouble determining the colour of the cat because of the light. It could have been brown or a musty grey. Colours change, he thought. It isn't only a matter of the eyes. It's a question of atmospheric conditions. What are colours anyway? Simply a refraction of light. Why does the sun sometimes look orange, sometimes yellow and sometimes mealy maroon? It hadn't changed physically. It was a trick brought on by different conditions in the upper reaches of orbital space – clouds, dust, water particles, magnetism, they all had their affect on the spectrum. The sun wasn't any particular colour – or rather it was all colours. So why were people so pernickety about the colour of his socks? Who cared if he called them green and they were, according to others, actually blue? (Of course, when one was green and the other blue he did become more noticeable and certain people did tend to point at him and snigger, but that was another issue,

he thought.)

There was a clicking sound and then the porch light went on, startling him. He didn't hear anyone coming to the door. The drapes were still closed around the front windows. Perhaps it was an automatic light, he thought, on a timing switch or triggered by the approaching dusk. He waited a moment, listening for sounds. Then, looking down, at his scuffed shoes, he lifted his foot, first the right and then the left, rubbing them against the side of his trousers while holding onto the doorknob for balance. He inspected them again. Didn't do much good, he thought. But at least he made the effort. They should appreciate that, shouldn't they? Well, perhaps not. How would they know? Scuffed shoes are scuffed shoes. Would they actually wonder whether he had rubbed them against his trousers in an attempt to make them less scuffed? Who in their right mind thinks of things like that?

But perhaps they're not in their right minds, he thought. What are right minds, in fact? The notion of 'right minds' implies minds that are not right. Therefore they're wrong – which brought him back to the colour question. Simply a matter of percentages. Right and wrong. Very relative. Einstein proved that, didn't he? Not about minds, of course, but it could have been. Who's to say that Einstein didn't first consider relativity as a matter of right minds or wrong ones?

He looked down at his shoes again and then wondered about his socks. Maybe he did have one green and one blue right now. He couldn't actually tell. The green socks were greenish blue and the blue socks were bluish green. How much green or how much blue it took to tilt them into the appropriate category was beyond him. If he had the money, he would have bought new socks – all green or all blue. Then he wouldn't have a problem. He'd throw the others away before he unwrapped the new ones. But he didn't have the money, so there was no point thinking about it. Besides, if he had all green socks or all blue socks, what would he do with his brown blazer which he desperately loved even though it was getting a bit threadbare? Couldn't he buy just a pair or two of brown socks to match? He thought about it for a moment and then shook his head. He didn't have any money anyway so why bother his brain with such complications?

He looked down at his shoes again. They really didn't look so bad, he thought. Not compared to a derelict he saw the other day who he had witnessed methodically carving a piece of old cardboard to fill a gaping hole in the bottom. The shoes were old army boots, he imagined. Maybe from the Second World War by the looks of them. What he thought most interesting was how the old man seemed to do the job of patching his boot with care, with … he considered the word carefully. What came to mind was 'tenderness'. Was that the word he was looking for? Perhaps not. He thought of his brown blazer which had been with him for more years than he could remember and how he was loath to throw it out even though some unkind soul had ac-cused it of smelling mildewed. So in a way he could understand the rumpled old fellow who seemed quite attached to his ancient boots even though who knows where they came from. Army boots were prob-ably worn by someone in the army, he thought. Therefore they had an aura of adventure, of danger, of.. (he smiled to himself, as if some great insight had been broached) ... youth. Well, it probably wasn't a great insight – a minor one, more likely. Whatever, major or minor, it was an insight none the less. The old man could have been a soldier and was attracted to the boots simply be-cause it reminded him of when he was young. But the boots were old, he remembered. Perhaps even as old as the man. Probably not, though. Leather doesn't last that long un-less someone is taking extra special care and rubbing it with softeners like neatsfoot oil and taking it to the shoe repair shop on a regular basis. The old man didn't seem the type to have done that. He clearly didn't have the capital for such expensive upkeep. So even though he might have been in the army when he was young, the boots probably weren't his then. They most likely belonged to anther soldier. In fact, they could have even belonged to another army. But what army? Rubbing his chin, he tried to recall the exact appearance of the boots and whether there was anything significant about them that might have denoted nationality. They were black, laceups with sixteen grommets, he estimated. The toe was rounded. He couldn't re-member anything else.

Suddenly he felt his left ear twitch. Was it his imagination or did he actu-ally hear creaking floor boards? He tried to listen as intently as he did back in his room when he was listen-ing for the dung beetle that lived, he suspected, under his bed and would come out at night when it thought he was asleep to munch on the news-paper clippings that filled several boxes stacked haphazardly on his floor. The more intently he listened the more certain he was that some-one was actually coming to the door. Of course, he felt that way about the dung beetle as well, only to be disappointed when he flung on the

lights hoping to catch the little bug-
ger in the act of actually devouring
his clippings in its miniscule jaws,
and slavering that ugly yellow juice
over the type making his clippings
even more difficult to decipher as
he had recently broken his reading
glasses and couldn't afford to have
them repaired just now. Unfortu-
nately he never caught it in its pro-
fane act. (He often wonder what he
would actually do if he did. He was
loath to kill it. And evicting it was
not something he could do without
a great deal of angst and anguish
as they had been roommates for so
long. He probably would have put it
in a box, the same kind he kept his
clippings in, and feed it adverts for

Toyota 4 by 4s – or something of the sort.)

As he was thinking of the dung beetle, trying to visualise it feasting on his cuttings, the door of putrid green swung open. At first, he wasn't sure he hadn't actually imagined it. Perhaps it was just an hallucination. He hadn't knocked. At least he didn't remember knocking. Maybe he had. He was becoming extraordinarily forgetful. So for a moment he simply stood there in a state that he later described as 'flusterment'.

'Yes? Can I help you?'

He squinted his eyes. There was a voice. He definitely heard a voice emanating from the space that the open door had provided. But it was dark inside. And his sight was far from perfect.

The voice spoke again. It was more insistent this time, 'Did you want something? Why are you here?'

'I .. eh … yes …' he stammered, trying to overcome his confusion.

'Yes? Yes what? What are you doing standing on my porch?'

He looked down at his shoes, his scuffy shoes. Indeed, he was standing on the porch and he assumed the porch he was standing on belonged to the invisible voice that was questioning him. But exactly why he was standing there suddenly escaped him.

'Speak up, young man!' the voice

bellowed - though 'bellow' isn't exactly the term he would have used to describe it had he time to think it out, which he did only later. Then he would have referred to the sound as rather forceful but not particularly loud (as 'bellow' would imply). In fact it was quite controlled and almost melodic in tone. And later he wondered whether the voice wasn't actually trained as an opera singer or, perhaps, an announcer on radio. But then it sounded pretty much like a bellow and it frightened him.

'I'm sorry,' he apologised. And then in a tone that could only be described as 'tremulous' (both then and later), he added, 'I'll go...'

But as he turned to go, the voice

called out to him. 'Wait!'

He turned back, now more con-fused than ever. And he looked in the voice's direction, questioningly.

'You forgot you valise,' the voice said.

'My valise?'

'Your attaché case, then.'

'Attaché case?'

'Well, what is that piece of luggage sitting on my porch?'

He looked back to where he had been standing and, indeed, there was a narrow rectangular box with a handle on the porch right where he had been. And it did look famil-iar.

'Ah, yes,' he said. 'My samples ...' He looked at it and nodded. 'My samples … of course.'

There was a moment of silence. Then the voice said, 'What are you waiting for?'

Looking around, he wondered the same thing himself. What was he waiting for? A bus? No, he didn't remember taking a bus here. How did he get there then? He didn't own a car. He didn't even have a license. In fact, he didn't know how to drive, having never actually been behind a steering wheel. No, he hated cars. And he definitely didn't come by taxi, because first, he couldn't afford it and second, he hated cars. Cars were the bane of his life, he would say to anyone who would listen (though most people wouldn't).   How much he would have rather come of age at a time when cars hadn't been invented and people got around by horse and buggy (though, he didn't trust horses after one had tried to eat his underwear). So, thinking about it, he must have walked. And if that were so, as it most likely was, he wasn't really waiting for anything. What should he reply, then?

Before he could think out his response, the voice called out again. 'Come up here and fetch your samples...'

He pointed to himself in a questioning manner and looked in the direction of the voice.

'Yes, you. Who else, for goodness

sakes!'

He let out a sigh. Of course, they were his samples, weren't they? Well not exactly. But they certainly weren't the voice's. It was up to him to collect them. That was clear enough. So, taking a deep breath, he ventured forward once more, several paces, climbing onto the porch and then, reaching down, taking the handle of the sample's case and, when it was firmly in his grasp, turning back around...

'Wait!' the voice called out.

Confused, he looked back toward the open door again.

'What do you have in the case?'

That was a very unexpected question, he thought. And it befuddled him. So he repeated it back, which is what he often did in times of confusion. 'What do I have in the case?'

'Yes, what do you have in the case? You said it was a samples case. What kind of samples do you have there?'

He scratched his head and looked down at the case. It did, indeed, look like an ordinary attaché case. Perhaps a little bigger. It was black and a bit scuffed, just like his shoes. And it had a wobbly handle. But what was inside of it? He was pretty sure he knew what was in it that morning when he had packed up to go. In fact, he was certain he knew then. But that was three or four hours ago, at least, and quite a few things had happened since he had left.

'Are you telling me that you don't know what kind of samples you have in your samples case?' asked the voice.

'I do know,' he replied. 'I'm thinking ...' And, indeed, he appeared to be putting a great deal of effort into that process which, for him, was most delicate.

The voice sighed. But it was a sympathetic sigh, he thought. Not one of those frustrating sighs of disapproval that he often heard when he got into one of his states of discombobulation (which was happening more and more frequently over the last twenty years).

The door of putrid green opened

wider. 'Would you like to come in?' asked the voice.

'Come in?' he repeated.

'Yes. Why don't you come inside and join me for a cherry soda. And you can show me your samples. Who knows? Maybe I'll find them interesting. Maybe I'll even find them interesting enough to buy one or two from you...'

'Buy one or two?' He now felt both dreadfully confused and anxious.

'I'm not promising anything, of course...'

'You want me to come in?' he asked, in order to confirm what he thought he heard but really wasn't quite sure.

'Yes.' The door opened even wider.

'Do come in.'

This was truly an amazing event, he thought. Quite beyond his wildest dreams. Here it was – the first house he had come to (at least he thought it was the first house he had come to) – and already he was being invited in to display his wares.

So, grabbing the handle of his samples case quite firmly, he bravely ventured forth into the unknown, though, it must be said, with a fluttering heart that would have competed easily with any butterfly hovering over a bee's nest.

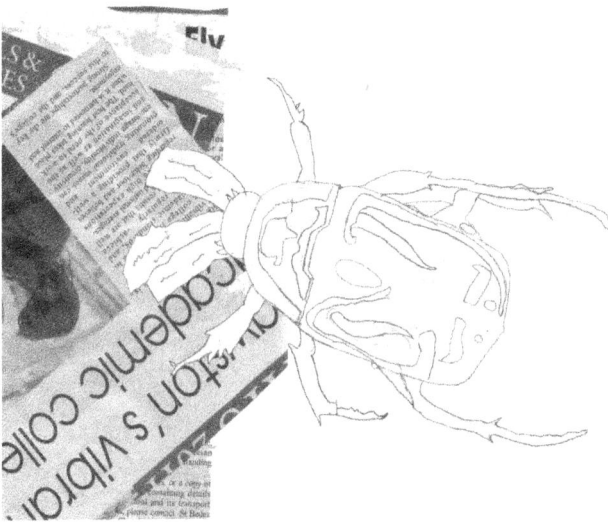

Name Change

Charles Morgan – what a name! Bog standard. And that's what he despised about it. He wanted to be different, but it was difficult being different with a name like Charles. And coupled with a surname like Morgan made it doubly impossible.

So he changed it. He went though the entire legal process of changing his name through deed poll. He accomplished this by going onto the web and Googling 'deed poll' + 'name change'. It was quick and easy. And the first site he came up with said:

"Welcome. If you wish to legally change your name, or your children's names, you can use the Deed Poll process, which has been used by hundreds of thousands of people for over 150 years. By Deed Poll, you can officially change any part or all of your name. For example, you can change your forenames, surname (or both), add names, remove names, change the spelling of your names or rearrange your existing forenames. You can change your name by Deed Poll as often as you want, at any time and for any reason provided it is not for deceptive or fraudulent purposes."

Intrigued by what he read, Charles Morgan contacted the Deed Poll agency and within weeks changed his first name to Hiram and his surname to Phumphnick.   Now why, you may ask.   Why change a perfectly good name like Charles Morgan to a rather odd one like Hiram Phumphnick?   The simple answer to this question is that Charles Morgan wanted to be odd.   And to be odd, he felt that he needed a name more suited to his oddity.   There is also a complicated answer, but the simple one will have to do for now.

Actually, the change of name worked wonders for him.   Prior to his name change, he felt both bored and boring.   Now, with his shiny new moniker he was not boring at all.   Nor was he bored.   Indeed, every time he introduced himself to someone, saying, 'Hello, my name is Hiram Phumphnick', he would get an interesting response rather than the jaded look when he had previous introduced himself as Charles Morgan. After all, a name like Charles Morgan is entirely shruggable. Whereas a name like Hiram Phumphnick makes people sit up and take notice - their facial muscles become more expressive, their eyebrows seem to lift, corners of mouths droop into whimsical frowns, eyes screw up in bemusement. And everything becomes simply more wonderful. Much more wonderful than being boring old Charles – according to Hiram, anyhow.

HIRAM

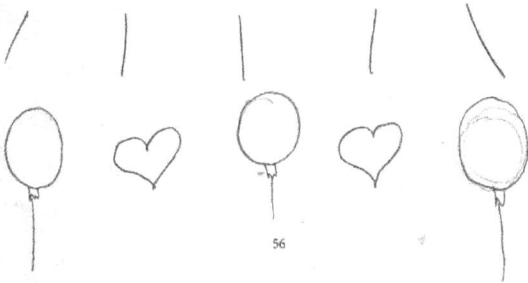

PHUMPHNICK!

56

Are we still in business?

Are we still in business?

I think so, but maybe not.

Will you check?

Yes, I'll check.

(There's a moment of silence and then a moment more).

Yes, we're still in business.

Are you sure?

No.

No?

No, I'm sure.

You're sure of what?

I'm sure we're not in business.

But I thought you said we were?

I did.

You did?

I did.

You did say that we're in business?

Yes.

So we are?

Yes, I think so.

But you don't know?

I knew once.

When?

Just a minute ago.

But then you said that you're sure we're not in business.

Of course.

Of course, what?

We are, as I said, not in business.

So we're not?

No.

We are?

Yes and no.

You mean maybe?

Perhaps that's the word for it, yes.

So (he sighs) we might be in business?

I would say that's closer to the mark.

(Grumbles) Can't you be more precise?

Precision is not my forte.

What is your forte, if I may be so bold to ask?

You may.

May what?

Be so bold to ask.

And will you answer?

Yes.

Well (starting to lose patience) then do!

Alright, if you insist.

I do insist!

My forte is…

Is what? Do go on. (Sarcastically)
Don't keep us in suspense!

Circumnavigation.

Circumnavigation?

Yes.

What does that mean?

It means my forte is circumnavigation.

Circumnavigating what?

Circumnavigation in all its forms.

Including reason, I suppose?

Yes.

So you admit you're not a reasonable man?

Yes. And that is why we're not in
business.

Because you're not reasonable?

Yes. And that's why we are.

Coffee Time

The phone rang just as he was spooning several heaping glugs of Camp into a big brown cup embossed with the picture of a clock grinning madly with wild eyes, its multiple hands pointing to the numbers 6, 8, 10, 12, 2 and 4. Underneath its maniacal leer, in letters of bold maroon was written, shakily (as if drawn by someone with severe astigmatism) the words, 'COFFEE TIME!'

Looking in the direction of the incessant ringing, he was aware that his reflexes had been short-circuited by caffeine deprivation and he was left in a state of immobility, not knowing whether to pour the water from the insistent kettle which had finally come to a gurgling boil into his crazed cup or to answer the infernal phone, each ring of which had become like a jackhammer pounding into his skull. Decisions like that defy logic. It is not one for pencil pushers or even the smug sophistication of a computer. It's more like the reaction of a mad dog when beset on one side by a smirking cat and on the other by a meaty bone. Does the canine ponder his options or simply react? And when he reacts, which way does he go?

Solomon being a man, and more intelligent (supposedly) than a dog, mad or not, went both ways at once, grabbing the phone with one hand and the boiling kettle with the other, splashing the hot water on himself as he frantically poured and shouting, 'Ow! Ow! Ow! God damn fucking shit!' into the receiver.

There was a deep, dark silence on the other end. Like the echoing nothingness one might encounter in an endless hole situated at the most distant, far off corner of the universe.

'Hello?' he repeated, with a bit more humility while under his breath he uttered one more 'shit!' very quietly as he felt his hand throb in pain because of its recent scalding.

'You haven't had your coffee yet, have you?' It was Daisy. Her voice was chastising.

'I'll call you back in a minute,' he said, ditching the phone. And running to the sink, he turned on the tap and stuck his wounded hand underneath the cooling waters.

The phone rang again with even more insistence than before. He let it ring (in the way a battered beast might respond to Pavlov's bell when finally realising, after years of abuse, that the whole thing was a set-up) and poured some water from the cooling kettle into the maniacal cup, stirring the brownish goo frantically until it dispersed its essence of chicory, sugar and coffee flavouring into the now muddy fluid before taking a greedy gulp and then, with a gagging noise that would have woken the dead if there were any dead to wake, spat what had regurgitated from his unwilling stomach back through his oesophagus and into the sink.

He remembered why he hated the stuff. And he blamed Napoleon.

Coffee? Napoleon? Waterloo? What are you thinking about now, you caffeine crazed idiot, he said to himself, as he tore through the shelves searching for a stash he might have hidden for days like today.

It was the Continental Blockade, Daisy had informed him – and, unlike most of what Daisy said, it had stuck in his head.

The French had all the pasta they wanted from Italy, all the olives from Greece, the oranges from Spain, all the herring from the Dutch – but the British ruled the waves and they impounded all the coffee from the Americas. What was Napoleon to do? His army might have lived on sour dough bread and liver pate but they marched on caffeine. And their chef source of the bean was coming from their plantations in the Caribbean whose shipments were impounded by the British fleet to Napoleon's dismay and eternal headache.

'The true history of the world is not made from battles and blood,' his father had told him in one of those rare moments of wisdom detached from his dreadfully long association with the military, 'those events are incidental. The real history of change and transition has to do with food and drink and bodily desires. If you want to know why things happened and why they didn't you need to look at the commodities – sugar, salt, oil, bread, wine and coffee. Who had what – and who didn't; that's all you need to know.'

When Napoleon found out he didn't have coffee in the state larder – at least enough to feed his grumpy soldiers – it was then he knew he was in very bad trouble. And that's when he discovered the bloody root.

Chicory! Roasted and ground it could increase the supply of coffee rations three or four or even six to one. The troops had their ersatz juice and Napoleon, briefly at least, was able to get them marching again.

Napoleon's chicory business, of course, was simply supposed to be a stopgap measure. But like many atrocious and artificial war-time foods created to replace short supplies of wholesomeness (think of SPAM!), the soldiers had acquired a taste for this treacle-like guck which, in their sordid nostalgia, became like swillish ambrosia. Thus had chicory remained a convenient additive, even after Napoleon was sent into exile, to the great delight of coffee merchants who were now able to cut their expensive import with cheap home-grown filler (anything brownish or black) similar to the way heroin dealers would later cut their product with inert starch, chalk or rat poison (anything white).

The phone rang again. He answered it. 'Sorry,' he apologised. 'I was in a fix...'

'You mean you needed a fix, don't you?' she replied. And without waiting for a response (if there was one in the offing – which, from experience, she doubted as he wasn't as quick on the uptake as she was), she continued, 'I've got you some translation work. Don't bother thanking me, just be at the Monmouth. 9 AM

- on the dot…'

'Whoa. Slow down, Daisy. What's this about?'

'Got to rush…'

'Who am I meeting?'

'The Egyptian…'

'The Egyptian?'

'Yes, you won't have any trouble recognising him. He always wears a fez…'

'If he's Egyptian, he'll be wearing a tarboosh…'

'What?'

'A tarboosh. Comes from the Persian - 'sar 'meaning head and 'poosh' meaning cover. It's almost the same - brimless, made of felt. But the tarboosh is cone-shaped. The fez is more rounded…'

'OK. I get the picture…'

'It's worn in Turkey…'

'The tarboosh?'

'No. The fez. The tarboosh is worn in Egypt…'

'I always called them 'fez' - all those cylindrical red hats topped with a tassel. Cute…'

'It's a tarboosh in Egypt. The fez was worn in Turkey. Until Atiturk banned them…'

'Why did he ban them? They're cute…'

'Because the Ottomans wore them and Atiturk was against everything the Ottomans were for…'

'Including the tarboosh?'

'Including the fez. There was something called the 'Hat Law' enacted in the mid 1920s...'

'Outlawing the fez?'

'Yeah. In the early 19th century Sultan Mahmud Khan II was keen on modernizing what was left of the Ottoman empire so he tried to get everyone to adopt European dress...'

'By wearing a fez?'

'By wearing suits instead of robes - but hats were trickier...'

'Why was that?'

'Because European hats had brims and Moslem men were supposed to prostrate themselves in prayer. So a brimless hat seemed better than a bowler. But then a hundred years later Ataturk went and banned them...'

'Solly!'

'What?'

'I've got to go…'

'Don't you want to know why the fez is so distinctly red?'

'Later. The Monmouth at 9. See the Egyptian with the fez…'

'You mean the tarboosh.'

'Yes, yes, whatever. Just be there!'

Daisy might have sounded abrupt to someone listening in, but she knew her customers. Solomon was an excellent translator (or so he was told) but a very poor businessman – which, for someone who depended on freelance assignments to make ends meet, was problematic. Daisy, however, was brilliant at organising other people's lives. And, as Solomon was terrible at organising his own, she was a perfect match for him – as long as he could keep her out of his kitchen and, in fact, out of his bedsit/office/studio. He preferred staying at her flat for their romantic interludes and then, after a day or two or three, vanishing back into his own inner world. Daisy, of course, resented this shutting out. But Solomon was the first man she ever found in her thirty-six and a half years on earth who was absolutely honest with her and could be both gentle and charming as well as a pain-in-the-neck (as were all men, according to her). What's more they had a nice, easy banter that could go on for hours concerning esoteric subjects that perhaps only seventeen people in the world would find interesting or worth more than a twenty second sound bite that could be switched off in ten. In short, Daisy and Solomon were two people well suited to each other – almost.

It was the 'almost' bit that caused them a certain amount of problems. But all things considered, it was a perfectly decent relationship, even if they did hang up on each other now and then.

Apes and Opera Singers

Solomon had a poster on his wall - an image of an ape side by side with Povarotti. Above, writ in 72 point embolden caps, was the question: 'Who are you?' Now that might, in some circles, have been considered rather adolescent, but Solomon, though not really fuelled by ontological obsessions, still considered it something that was slightly on his mind ever since he was old enough to entertain the idea that he might actually be someone – but who? He had a name given to him by his parents; he had a birth certificate, a vaccination certificate, a National Insurance card with his unique number embossed across the front; a degree from a semi-prestigious university and a post doctorate from a slightly more celebrated one. But who was he? The ape or the opera singer?

'You're neither,' Daisy reminded him.

'I'm both,' he corrected her.

'You've never sung opera in your life,' she said. 'Though I admit you eat a lot of bananas.'

'How do you know?' he asked, raising his left eyebrow.

'That you eat bananas or that you've never sung an aria?'

'That I've never sung an aria.'

'Well sing me one, then,' she said, in that challenging tone of hers which might well have launched a thousand prima donnas.

'I don't know any at the moment,' he admitted. 'But that doesn't mean I didn't sometime in the past...'

'In this life or another?' she queried, looking at him with the same suspicious eyelids-narrowed, searchlight stare that made him quiver.

'In this one. I like singing in the shower.'

'What?'

'What, what?'

'What do you like to sing?'

'Something from The Barber of Seville...'

'Go on, sing it then...'

'I don't know the words.'

'Then hum.'

He took a deep breath and hummed.

'That's awful!' she said, wrinkling up her nose. 'Truly, madly awful. In fact it give a new meaning to aw-fulness.'

'I didn't say I was good,' he replied.

'So you're not an opera singer.'

'You don't have to be good to be an opera singer,' he corrected. 'You just have to sing opera...'

'But you weren't singing.'

'I was.'

'You were humming.'

'Humming is a sort of singing, isn't it? The accepted definition of the verb "to sing" is the act of making musical sounds with the voice. It doesn't necessitate the use of words...'

'It's the notion of "musicality" I think that's problematic,' she replied.

'The word "music" derives from "mousik", he said, 'a Greek word which means "the art of the muse". No actual muse is specified.'

'So it might be the muse of bad singing?' She thought about that for a moment. Then, looking back at him sweetly, with child-like eyes ('Uh, oh,' he thought, 'here it comes...'). 'If I understand what you're saying, you – who admits to knowing not a single libretto, and has a voice that would send chills down the quills of a porcupine, are...' (and here she pointed back to the poster on the wall) '... an opera singer somewhat similar to Pavoratti...'

'I didn't say "similar to"...'

'Your poster sort of implies it.'

'The question you asked me, some-time ago...' (How long had it been – seconds, minutes, decades – ages!) '... had to do with whether I saw myself as an ape or an opera singer because the poster which you refer to has a print of a commonly accept-ed image of each, of both, though it could have simply had the words "Ape" and "Opera Singer" instead of pictures and then you would have had to supply the image yourself, in your mind's eye, so you might have substituted the ape you last saw when you went to the zoo …'

'I don't go to zoos,' she interrupted. 'I don't like the idea of animals being kept in cages...'

'Good zoos don't keep them in cages anymore...'

'Animals should be in the jungle where they belong...'

'The jungles are disappearing. Something to do with climate change and the never-ending quest for resources...'

'Which is why I'm always so pissed off at you when you don't recycle your rubbish!'

He closed his eyes and held up his hand, realising that if he let this conversation go so far afield they'd soon end up in China and back to the debate on the origin of green tea which took up an entire evening last month.

'Could we rewind?' he asked.

'Back to where?' she replied.

'Back to when I said, "...in your mind's eye, so you might have substituted..."'

'Ok, but leave out the zoo.'

He sighed. 'Alright...' Then, taking an all-suffering deep breath, he continued, 'The picture of Povaratti was meant to be that of a generic opera singer and was used because he is so easily recognisable. So you were meant to think "opera singer" not "Povaratti" when you saw the picture. Just like you were meant to think "ape" in general rather than a specific one...'

'I don't know any specific apes...'

'You don't know Povaratti, either,' he reminded her.

'But I do know the picture of the opera singer refers to an actual person. The picture of the ape doesn't...'

He went over and inspected the ape image more closely. It wasn't a drawing but a photo – probably cut out from a larger scene. From the jungle or the zoo? 'It probably is a specific ape,' he said. 'We just don't know him...'

'Or her.'

'Our eyes aren't trained to recognise specificities in apes. A picture of an ape is simply an ape but one of an opera singer is more defined. We know the ape is an ape because of its shape, its stance, its general appearance but we wouldn't know an opera singer except by some reference to a person who we know to sing opera.'

She let that regurgitate for a moment before replying because even before she put it together in her head, something didn't sound right. 'You're not comparing like with like,' she said. 'You could either contrast ape and human, in which case you would have two general representations of specific species or you could compare banana eater and opera singer…"

'All apes eat bananas. Not all humans are opera singers,' he said.

'From your definition of "opera singer" I suspect that all humans are.'

'Well, how do we know that all apes eat bananas?' he replied.

There was a sudden look of confusion in her face. Did she actually know all apes ate bananas? Or was it just another case of clichéd generalisation – something she detested. 'I think it's still OK, what I said…' she mumbled, looking at him anxiously.

He took her hand, seeing that she needed reassurance. Maybe this had gone too far. 'No. You're right. All apes eat bananas.'

'But what if one was shipwrecked

on a desert island…'

'Shipwrecked?'

'You know, a jungle ape snatched from its habitat and put on a ship bound for the New York zoological gardens. Suddenly there's a force ten hurricane. The ship is caught up in a ferocious storm and smashed against a gigantic reef…'

'Where?'

'Where what?

'Where is the reef it smashed up against?'

'I don't know. Somewhere between the Caribbean and Boston harbour, I expect…'

He nodded. 'Ok. Go on…'

She blinked her eyes, having really been caught up in the story of this ape seized from the wilds, torn from the arms of its loyal mate, heartlessly separated from its children and the banana trees it so deeply loved and admired...

'Poor Harry!' she sobbed.

'Harry?'

'The shipwrecked ape,' she explained.

'He has a name?'

She looked at him as if he had been the ape snatcher, himself. 'Why shouldn't he have a name? The opera singer has a name, doesn't he?'

'Yes. But what's the point you're making?'

'Point? Oh, yes, there was a point. Let me think...'

'Actually, things don't really have

to have a point…'

'Yes they do!'

'So what is it?'

Then it flashed into her head - ding, dong! Of course! There is a point! 'If the ape was on a desert island – a desert island without banana trees but lots of other fruit, like apples, pears, persimmons, avocados – would it survive? And if it did, could we still say all apes eat bananas?'

'Maybe that's the exception that proves the rule,' he suggested.

'I never really understood that expression,' she said, looking at him curiously. 'Why not say that's the rule that proves the exception?'

'I was just trying to be helpful. You

seemed to be so caught up in your story. I simply wanted to give it a happy ending, that's all…'

'By telling me that's the exception that proves the rule? Either all apes eat bananas or not all apes eat bananas. One is true, both aren't.'

'There's always an exception,' he told her.

'Always?'

'Always.'

'How about, 'All people need to breath air or else they'll turn blue.'

'You see? That itself is an exception.'

'To what?'

'To the statement, "There's always an exception."'

She blinked at him once and then

twice and then twice more.

Later that evening he did a bit of research on shipwrecked apes. He found reference to a rather bizarre case during the Napoleonic wars of a French galleon sunk off the coast of Hartlepool. The citizens anxiously waited to see if there were any survivors. As there was only one, he was captured and immediately hung as a form of summary justice meted out to enemy sailors who dared step foot on English soil. Only later was it pointed out to the good people of Hartlepool that the enemy sailor was actually an ape that had been kept as the ship's mascot. When questioned, the townsfolk admitted the survivor looked a little strange but, then again, they had never seen a Frenchman.

Reading that bit of fantastic history caused him to scratch the mole on his forehead as he recalled that sometime ago he had come to the conclusion that all true history was bizarre – the rest, the reams of books full of battles, dates and infinite varieties of statistical data, were the kind of fluff that both pillows and schoolboy minds were stuffed with. But that thought was quickly supplanted by another and the new one concerned the mole he was scratching (molesting?) out of habit. This particular mole was on his forehead right beside the tip of his eyebrow that pointed uneasily toward his left ear.   And realising he was scratching it, even though he knew he shouldn't, made him think of moles and that made him wonder how many things he could think about before he stopped thinking – full stop – like a bucket filled with water that couldn't take any more without sloshing over the top and onto the wooden floor causing both a mess and a predicament for the grumpy neighbour who lived below him.